The New England Colonies
A Place for Puritans

Kelly Rodgers

Consultants

Katie Blomquist
Fairfax County Public Schools

Nicholas Baker, Ed.D.
Supervisor of Curriculum and Instruction
Colonial School District, DE

Publishing Credits

Rachelle Cracchiolo, M.S.Ed., *Publisher*
Conni Medina, M.A.Ed., *Managing Editor*
Emily R. Smith, M.A.Ed., *Series Developer*
Diana Kenney, M.A.Ed., NBCT, *Content Director*
Johnson Nguyen, *Multimedia Designer*
Lynette Ordoñez, *Editor*

Image Credits: Cover and p. 1 LOC [LC-DIG-pga-00346]; pp. 2–3, 4–5, 9, 11–17, 20, 22, 23–25, 27–28, 32 North Wind Picture Archives; p. 6 Yale University Art Gallery, New Haven, CT, USA/Bridgeman Images; p. 7 Historical Documents Co.; p. 8 Chicago Architectural Sketch Club Collection, Ryerson and Burnham Archives, The Art Institute of Chicago Digital File #casc.1923_134.; p. 9 Courtesy of the Webb-Deane-Stevens Museum, photo by Charles Lyle; pp. 10, 17–19 Granger, NYC; p. 11 LOC [74692168]; p. 14 LOC [mc0023_01]; p. 18 Mary Evans Picture Library/Alamy; p. 19 Beinecke Rare Book and Manuscripts Library, Yale University; p. 23 Public domain; all other images from iStock and/or Shutterstock.

Library of Congress Cataloging-in-Publication Data

Names: Rodgers, Kelly, author.
Title: The New England colonies : a place for Puritans / Kelly Rodgers.
Description: Huntington Beach, CA : Teacher Created Materials, 2016. | Includes index. | Audience: Grades 4 to 6.?
Identifiers: LCCN 2015051147 (print) | LCCN 2016003525 (ebook) | ISBN 9781493830756 (pbk.) | ISBN 9781480756779 (eBook)
Subjects: LCSH: New England--History--Colonial period, ca. 1600-1775--Juvenile literature.
Classification: LCC F7 .R675 2016 (print) | LCC F7 (ebook) | DDC 974/.02--dc23
LC record available at http://lccn.loc.gov/2015051147

Teacher Created Materials
5301 Oceanus Drive
Huntington Beach, CA 92649-1030
http://www.tcmpub.com
ISBN 978-1-4938-3075-6

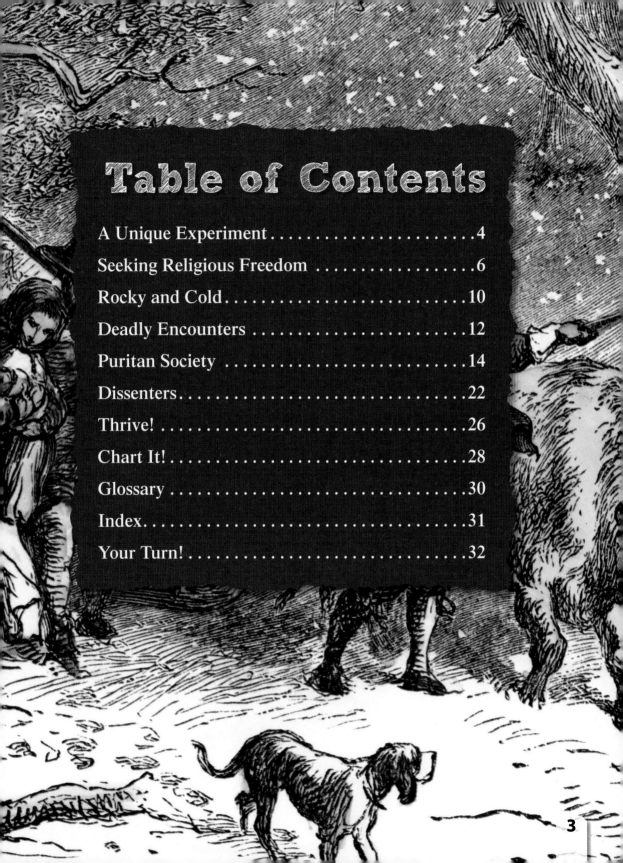

Table of Contents

A Unique Experiment 4

Seeking Religious Freedom 6

Rocky and Cold. 10

Deadly Encounters 12

Puritan Society 14

Dissenters. 22

Thrive! 26

Chart It! 28

Glossary 30

Index. 31

Your Turn! 32

A Unique Experiment

English interest in North America was on the rise in the early 1600s. The men who sponsored settlement wanted to make money fast. Many hoped to find gold. But several early **colonies** had failed. Settlers had not been prepared for the challenges of life in the New World.

In the 1620s, a new group of colonists came to America. These colonists wanted **religious** freedom. Their leaders advised them to work together. This was the only way to survive.

Colonists arrive in New England.

Colonists worked hard. They built towns, farmed, and started businesses. They freely practiced their religion. But no one knew if they would succeed. They faced many problems. Half of them died in the first winter. Their once friendly relations with the American Indians became hostile. More conflicts emerged as colonists were not accepting of each other's differences. Yet some problems led to improvements. New colonies were established, and strong traditions for independence were born. The story of New England is the story of a unique **experiment**.

Seeking Religious Freedom

In England during the early 1600s, some people wanted to reform, or change, the Church of England. They thought the Church of England was too much like the Roman Catholic Church. They wanted to "purify" it of Catholic practices. These people became known as **Puritans**. Puritans were told they had to conform to the Church of England. Some were put in jail. So they decided to leave England. They hoped to form a "New England" where they could practice their religion freely.

One group of Puritans wanted to completely separate itself from the church. The group became known as *Separatists* or **Pilgrims**. Pilgrim leader William Bradford asked the Virginia Company for a **charter**. The charter granted the Pilgrims land for a new settlement.

In 1620, the Pilgrims set sail on the *Mayflower*. They headed for the Virginia colony, but their ship went off course. They landed hundreds of miles away, near Cape Cod.

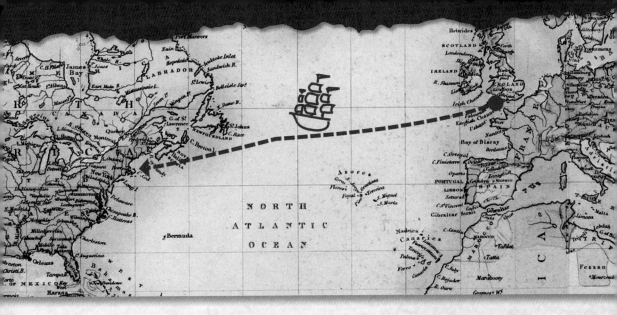

Before leaving their ship, the men discussed how they would be **governed**. They pledged their loyalty to the king of England. They decided the government in their new colony, which they called Plymouth, would be based on just laws. All laws would be made "for the general good of the colony." Their agreement was called the Mayflower Compact.

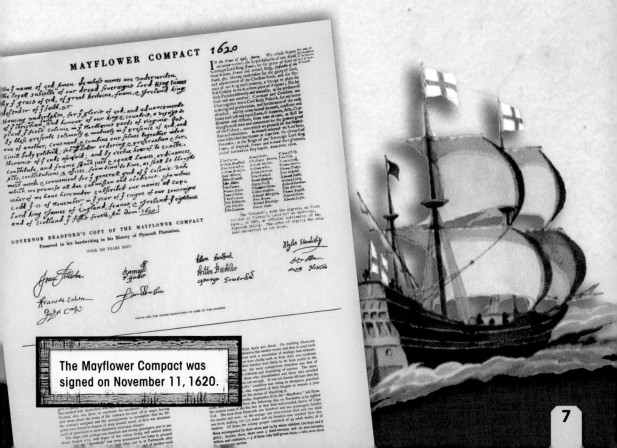

The Mayflower Compact was signed on November 11, 1620.

The Puritans faced more problems in England. Another Puritan leader, John Winthrop, decided to leave England and sail to the New World. There, he hoped to create a model society. A business called the Massachusetts Bay Company was given a charter to start a new colony. Winthrop joined them to start his new society.

In 1630, Winthrop and around 1,000 colonists set sail. Winthrop traveled on a ship called the *Arabella*. He spoke to those on board. He explained his vision for the new colony. According to Winthrop, the colonists would need to be faithful to their beliefs. They would have to work together in order to survive. Winthrop hoped the new colony would become an example of a perfect community. He said the new society should strive to be a "city upon a hill."

Winthrop's ships landed in Salem. The colonists settled along the Charles River. There, they established the city of Boston. Now, there were two new settlements—one at Plymouth and the other at Massachusetts Bay. A "New England" had been born.

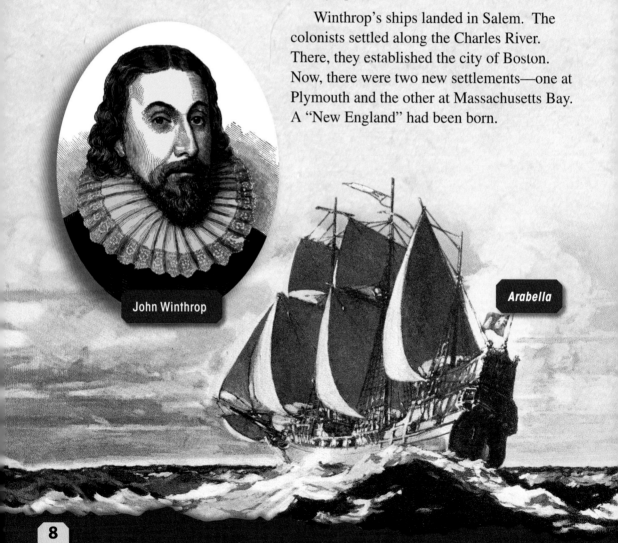

John Winthrop

Arabella

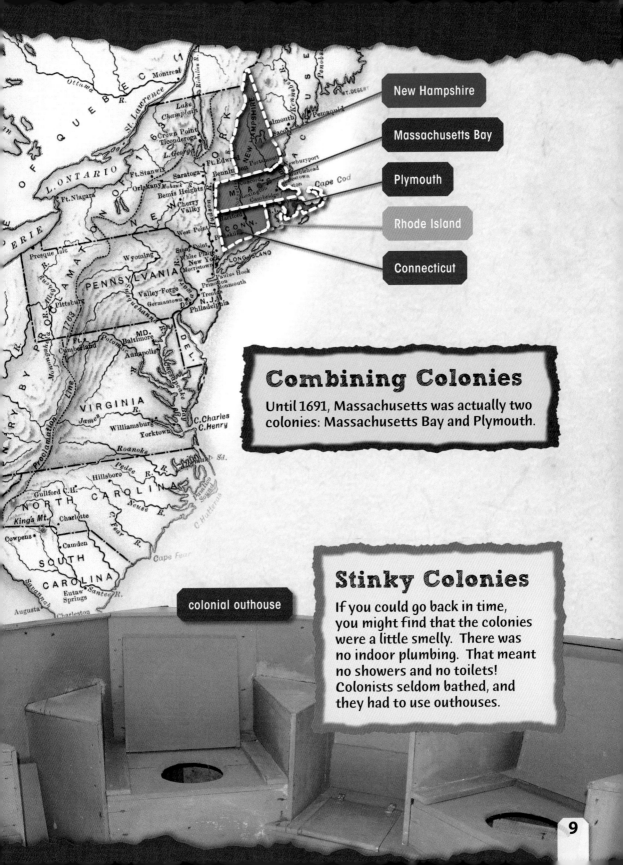

New Hampshire

Massachusetts Bay

Plymouth

Rhode Island

Connecticut

Combining Colonies

Until 1691, Massachusetts was actually two colonies: Massachusetts Bay and Plymouth.

colonial outhouse

Stinky Colonies

If you could go back in time, you might find that the colonies were a little smelly. There was no indoor plumbing. That meant no showers and no toilets! Colonists seldom bathed, and they had to use outhouses.

Rocky and Cold

Land and climate played an important role in New England. The northern climate was cool. The growing season was short. The soil was rocky and not very **fertile**. This made farming difficult. Strong houses and thick clothing were needed.

But there were advantages, too. The cooler climate meant fewer disease-carrying insects. Because of the climate, New England colonists lived longer and healthier lives. They often lived beyond 70 years of age. In the southern colonies, the expected life span was only around 45 years.

There were many natural resources, too. This supported many different types of **industries**.

The Pilgrims land at Plymouth Rock in December of 1620.

A colonial family travels to the Connecticut Valley in the 1630s.

New colonists continued to pour in. In 1623, settlers began moving into New Hampshire. By 1679, New Hampshire was a royal province. In 1636, Thomas Hooker led colonists to form a settlement at Hartford. Other leaders created New Haven. These towns soon became the Connecticut colony. Despite being rocky and cold, New England prospered and grew.

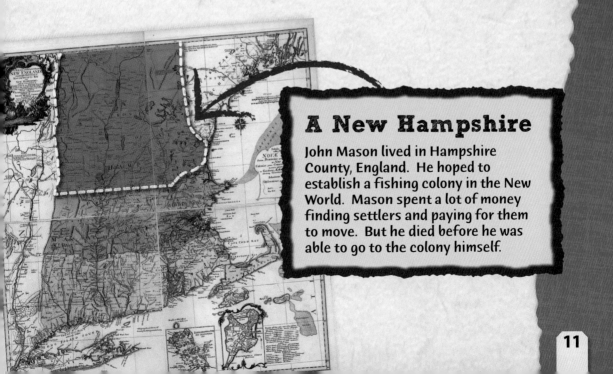

A New Hampshire

John Mason lived in Hampshire County, England. He hoped to establish a fishing colony in the New World. Mason spent a lot of money finding settlers and paying for them to move. But he died before he was able to go to the colony himself.

Deadly Encounters

New England was not an empty place when colonists arrived. Many American Indians lived there. As colonists cleared the land, tribes felt threatened. Colonists did not always treat American Indians fairly. There were **disputes** over land use. These disputes led to wars.

In 1634, colonists kidnapped and killed an American Indian from the Pequot (PEE-kwaht) tribe. The tribe attacked the colonists in return. The back and forth fighting became known as the Pequot War. In 1637, colonists surrounded a Pequot fort along the Mystic River. More than 500 Pequot were killed.

The English attack Block Island during the Pequot War.

In 1675, another war broke out. The Wampanoag (wahm-puh-NOH-ag) tribe, led by Chief Metacom, was angry. Colonists had been taking over more and more of the tribe's land. They had also killed three tribal members. Metacom (known as King Philip to the colonists) organized several tribes to fight. This became known as King Philip's War. The brutal dispute lasted over a year and led to many tragedies. Disease spread among the tribes. There were food shortages. Tribes could not compete with the colonists' weapons. But both sides paid a high price for these deadly encounters. After this war, colonists took control of the region.

Chief Metacom

A
RELATION OR
Iournall of the beginning and proceedings
of the English Plantation setled at *Plimoth* in NEW
ENGLAND, by certaine English Aduenturers both
Merchants and others.

With their difficult passage, their safe ariuall, their
ioyfull building of, and comfortable planting them-
selues in the now well defended Towne
of NEW PLIMOTH.

AS ALSO A RELATION OF
seuerall discoueries since made by some
same English Planters there resident.

I. In a iourney to PVCKANOKICK the habitation of t
test King Massasoyt : as also their message, the answer an
they had of him.
II. In a voyage made by ten of them to the Kingdome of
a boy that had lost himselfe in the woods : with such accide
in that voyage.
III. In their iourney to the Kingdome of Namascnet, i
greatest King Massasoyt, against the Narrohiggonsets,
supposed death of their Interpreter Tisquantum.
IIII. Their voyage to the Massachusets, and their ent

With an answer to all such obiections as are any way made
against the lawfulnesse of English plantations
in those parts.

Thanksgiving

Relations with American Indians weren't always hostile. According to a letter from Edward Winslow (left), after the harvest, the governor called for a celebration. Winslow writes that many American Indians joined in the three-day feast in 1621. Many people believe this was the first Thanksgiving.

Puritan Society

Life in the colonies was very different than life in England. And Puritans made a society all their own.

Town System

The New England colonies were not the richest colonies. But by 1700, they were the most populous. Leaders of the New England colonies gave land to groups of men who then formed towns. Most farmed the land to provide food for their families.

THE GENERALL
LAWS
OF THE *MASSACHUSETS*
COLONY.
REVISED AND PUBLISHED, BY
ORDER OF THE
GENERAL COURT

This 1672 document lists laws for the Massachusetts Bay colony.

Boston, Massachusetts in the 1600s

first Church in New England

People living in the towns supported one another. They made a covenant, or promise, to the people of the town. They promised to obey the word of God. They promised to do what was best for the people. Each town built its own church. Church attendance was required. Towns established schools, too.

Each town made its own government. In town meetings, men who owned property **elected** local leaders. Townsmen discussed problems and made decisions. This town system helped the Puritans keep order in their society. During town and church meetings, people learned about their responsibilities to the community.

Family Life

Unlike Virginia colonists who were mostly men, Puritans came to America as families. This helped the colonies succeed. Families were better able to deal with the challenges of life on a farm. New England families could not afford servants or slaves. They were **self-reliant**. They depended mostly on themselves to do the work.

All family members had responsibilities. Men farmed, cleared land, built houses and barns, and took care of livestock. Women took care of the home and cared for the children. They also made clothing and prepared food. Children helped their parents. Boys worked alongside their fathers. Girls helped their mothers with household chores.

A woman churns milk into butter.

Puritans are publicly punished in the stocks.

Puritan values were very strict. The entire community watched over everyone else. If town members thought that parents were not disciplining their children, they could step in. They could take children from their homes and place them with others families. If people did not go to church, they were punished. Often, the community disciplined people in public. Sometimes, they were placed in **stocks** in the town square. The Puritans believed this was the way to keep order and be successful.

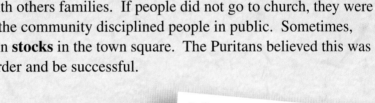

This book from the Bible was printed in Massachusetts in 1640.

Reading Rules!

Today, reading is an important skill. And it was a big part of Puritan life, too. They believed that all people should read the Bible. Even children who did not attend school were still expected to read.

THE

VVHOLE
BOOKE OF PSALMES
Faithfully
TRANSLATED *into* ENGLISH
Metre.

Whereunto is prefixed a difcourfe de-
claring not only the lawfullnes, but alfo
the neceffity of the heavenly Ordinance
of finging Scripture Pfalmes in
the Churches of
God.

Coll. III.
Let the word of God dwell plenteoufly in
you, in all wifdome, teaching and exhort-
ing one another in Pfalmes, Himnes,

17

Puritan Women

In New England society, men and women had different roles. Women managed the daily lives of their families. The most important role for a woman was being a mother. Most Puritan women had large families with many children. It was their duty to raise and educate their children. Though many Puritan children attended school, **moral** values were taught at home.

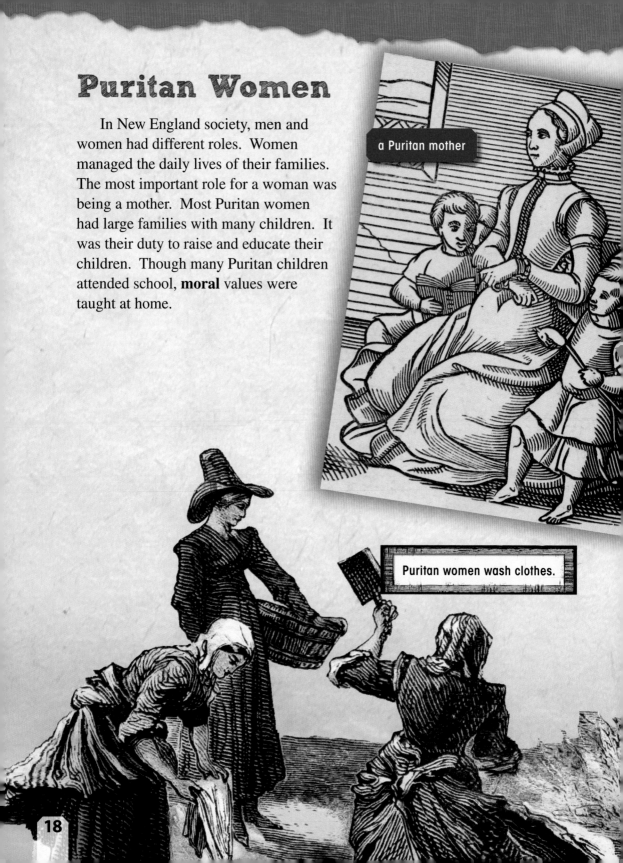

a Puritan mother

Puritan women wash clothes.

THE TENTH MUSE
Lately fprung up in AMERICA.
OR
everall Poems, compiled
with great variety of VVit
and Learning, full of delight.
rein efpecially is contained a com-
eat difcourfe and defcription of
Four { Elements,
{ Conftitutions,
{ Ages of Man,
{ Seafons of the Year.
ner with an Exact Epitomie of
the Four Monarchies, viz.
The { Affyrian,
{ Perfian,
{ Grecian,
{ Roman.
lo a Dialogue between Old England and
New, concerning the late troubles.
man in thofe part*.
hen Bowtell at the figne of the
Hed-Alley. 1650.

Anne Bradstreet and
her book of poems

Anne Bradstreet

Anne Bradstreet came to New England with her family on the *Arabella*. Though not formally educated, she wrote a book of poems. It is the first published poetry written in America. The poems are well known to this day.

The Puritans borrowed ideas about gender roles from English society. Women did not have much freedom. Men dominated public life in New England. When Puritan women married, they gave up their legal rights to their husbands. Married women could not own property. They could not enter into contracts. They could not use the courts to help settle disputes. Women could not vote. They could not hold public office. They could not become ministers.

Because Puritans lived in small towns, women supported each other. They gathered together to share information and news. They helped each other through childbirth and sickness. They were there for each other during hard times.

Making a Living

New England had growing pains for a number of years. During the early 1630s, colonists and money poured in. But as time passed, fewer colonists arrived. An economic **depression** settled in. Colonists worked hard to develop new industries. They wanted to bring life back to New England.

In the past, most farmers only produced enough crops to feed their own families. But colonists soon started growing crops for export. Wheat, rye, and barley were traded to other colonies. Dairy products such as butter and cheese, and meat such as beef and pork were traded, too. Maple syrup and furs were important trade products as well.

Pilgrims plant seeds in the 1620s.

Whaling

In colonial times, many products were made from whales. Whale oil was used for lighting and for lubricating machines. Bones were used to make skirts and umbrellas. Today, whaling is illegal in the United States.

Whalers harpoon a sperm whale.

Many new businesses grew in New England. Timber became a thriving industry. This allowed shipbuilding to flourish as well. Shipbuilding brought in skilled workers such as **shipwrights** and sailors. But the most important new industry was fishing. The fishing industry boomed. Fish were shipped to Europe and the West Indies. Soon, the New England economy became very **diverse**. The economy did not depend on just one crop or product, but on many.

These new trades brought more people to New England. Many were not Puritans. The Puritans struggled to keep their power in the growing towns and cities.

Dissenters

The plan to create a model society was not realistic. Puritans came to America for religious freedom. But they were not **tolerant**. They did not allow anyone to practice a different religion. Church leaders and town leaders were usually the same people. They made laws about daily life and religion. And they punished those who broke them. Soon, several Puritan leaders spoke out.

One such leader was Roger Williams. He said the Puritans had made mistakes. Williams did not think colonists should take land from American Indians. He thought they should buy the land. He was also angry about the power of town leaders. Town leaders could punish people for their religious beliefs. Williams thought that governing power and church power should be separate.

Roger Williams arrives in Rhode Island.

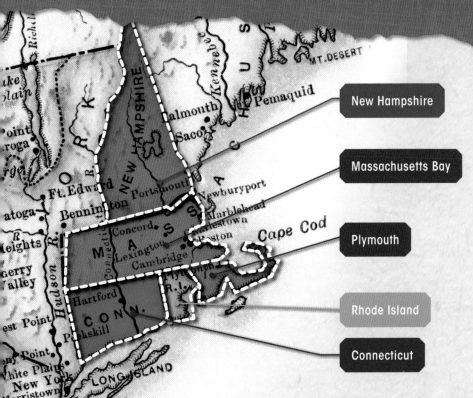

New Hampshire

Massachusetts Bay

Plymouth

Rhode Island

Connecticut

Williams's ideas made people mad. He was forced to leave his town. He and his followers moved south. They bought land from the Narragansett Indians. They made a new colony there. They called it Rhode Island. They established religious freedom and tolerance in Rhode Island. They made the powers of church and state separate.

Adriaen Block

Roodt Eylandt

The original name for Rhode Island was "Roodt Eylandt." It was named by Dutch explorer Adriaen Block. It means "Red Island" in Dutch. Block named the land for the red clay along the waterways. Later, when the British took over Dutch territories in North America, the name was changed.

Anne Hutchinson was another **dissenter**. Hutchinson led neighbors and friends in prayer at her home. She thought that people who believed in God could worship on their own. She did not think a minister was needed to interpret the Bible. Hutchinson was a threat to the power of men. And she disobeyed church law by teaching her ideas about the Bible. Like Williams, Puritan leaders banished her. Hutchinson went to Rhode Island. Later, she moved to New Amsterdam, a Dutch colony.

The General Court of Massachusetts sentences Anne Hutchinson in 1637.

Soon, the Puritans had more problems. There was much suspicion and tension in Puritan towns. These feelings grew because of the limits placed on women. People were often fearful. They were afraid they would be punished. Belief in magic was common. Sometimes, magic was the only explanation people had for natural events. Puritans became afraid of witchcraft. In 1692, in the town of Salem, a group of women were accused of being witches. Fear grew into panic. More than 150 people were arrested. Of these, 19 were hanged. The panic over witchcraft eventually died out. But the Salem Witch Trials became **infamous**.

A woman is arrested for being a witch.

This image shows Tituba as a witch.

Tituba

In February 1692, two girls in Salem became ill. One girl barked like a dog, ran a high fever, and screamed in pain. Doctors accused Tituba, the family's slave, of witchcraft. When questioned, Tituba confessed. She was sent to jail but was never tried. Later, she was released and disappeared.

Thrive!

By 1636, New England included four colonies. Colonists continued to face many challenges. This region was founded to be a refuge from life in England. Puritans hoped to build a "city upon a hill." This may not have been a realistic dream. But the colonists worked hard. They were resourceful. They became self-reliant. The Puritans believed strongly in education. Most learned to read and write as children. They founded schools and universities. Harvard College opened in 1636. Its goal was to train ministers. Today, it is one of the top schools in the country. Puritan values played an important role in shaping America.

Harvard today

Colonists buy goods from a shop.

New Englanders built a thriving economy. They did not become dependent on any one product. Merchants prospered. This meant success for the colonies. But England was not happy. The colonies were founded to help the mother country. New England's independence and success was a threat to English power. Soon, this conflict would lead to a war that would change the world.

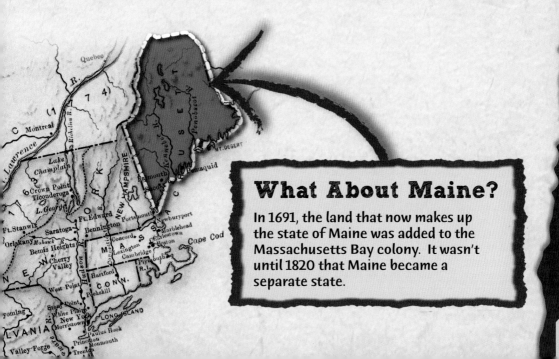

What About Maine?

In 1691, the land that now makes up the state of Maine was added to the Massachusetts Bay colony. It wasn't until 1820 that Maine became a separate state.

Chart It!

There were five colonies in New England. They were Massachusetts Bay, Plymouth, New Hampshire, Connecticut, and Rhode Island. Each colony was founded at a different time. They were founded and lived in by different people, too. Each colony formed a unique economy.

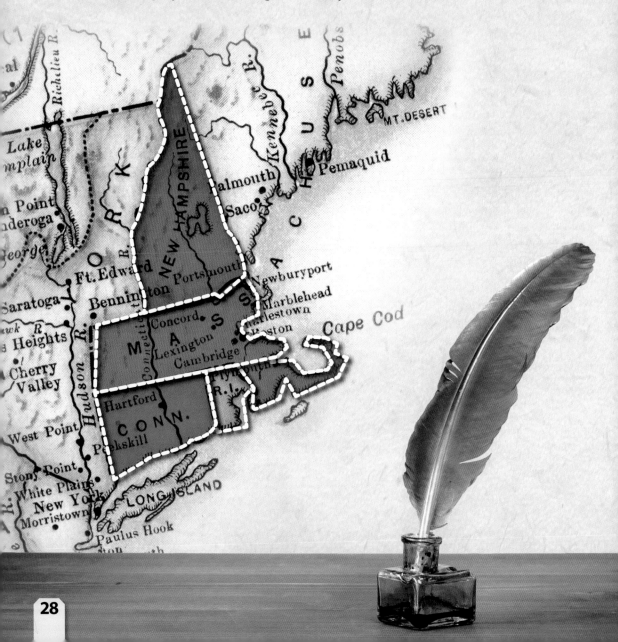

Research the New England colonies. Use this book as well as other sources to find information. Make a chart like the one below. Compare the colonies in your chart. Discuss with a friend how the colonies were the same and different.

	Massachusetts (Massachusetts Bay and Plymouth)	New Hampshire	Connecticut	Rhode Island
Year Founded				
Founder				
Location				
Economy				
Interesting Facts				

Glossary

charter—a document issued by the king giving land to the colonists

colonies—areas that are controlled by or belong to a country far away

depression—a period of time in which there is little economic activity and many people do not have jobs

disputes—disagreements or arguments

dissenter—a person who publicly disagrees with an official opinion, decision, or set of beliefs

diverse—made up of things that are different from each other

elected—chosen by voting

experiment—a test to see how well something will work

fertile—able to support the growth of many plants

governed—officially controlled or lead; ruled

industries—groups of businesses that provide a particular product or service

infamous—well known for being bad

moral—concerning or relating to what is right and wrong in human behavior

Pilgrims—Protestants who wished to separate from the Church of England

Puritans—members of a Protestant group in the 16th and 17th centuries that opposed many customs of the Church of England

religious—believing in a god or a group of gods and the following of rules associated with that belief

self-reliant—not needing help from other people

shipwrights—people who build and repair ships

stocks—wooden frames with holes in them for a person's feet, hands, or head that were used as a form of punishment

tolerant—willing to accept feelings, habits, or beliefs that are different from your own

Index

Arabella, 8, 19

Block, Adriaen, 23

Boston, 8, 14

Bradford, William, 6

Bradstreet, Anne, 19

Cape Cod, 6

Chief Metacom, 13

Connecticut, 9, 11, 23, 28–29

Hartford, 11

Harvard College, 26

Hooker, Thomas, 11

Hutchinson, Anne, 24, 32

King Philip's War, 13

Maine, 27

Mason, John, 11

Massachusetts Bay colony, 8–9, 14, 27–29

Massachusetts Bay Company, 8

Mayflower, 6

Mayflower Compact, 7

New Hampshire, 9, 11, 23, 28–29

New Haven, 11

Pequot, 12

Pequot War, 12

Plymouth, 7–9, 23, 28–29

Rhode Island, 9, 22–24, 28–29

Salem, 8, 25

Tituba, 25

Virginia Company, 6

Wampanoag, 13

Williams, Roger, 22–24

Winslow, Edward, 13

Winthrop, John, 8

Your Turn!

Banished!

In this image, Anne Hutchinson is banished from the Massachusetts colony. How would you describe her reaction and the reactions of the other colonists? Write what she and the other colonists might be thinking.